MAKE MONEY WITH ZERO COST

THE NO-COST SECRET TO ONLINE WEALTH

By Benjamin Lang

Table of Contents

Foreword

Disclaimer

Introduction

Understanding Digital Products Arbitrage

Platforms for Arbitrage

Effective Strategies for Reselling

Kickstarting Your Digital Arbitrage Journey

Specific Products and Services for Arbitrage

Advanced Techniques and Tips

Risk Management and Safety

Setting Up Your Business

Scaling Your Business

Conclusion

FOREWORD

Hey there,

If you're reading this, chances are you're in a bit of a financial pinch, right? Maybe you've been scouring the internet for an easy way to make some money, but nothing's really panned out. You've probably bought your fair share of books or courses, all promising to be the golden ticket, but here you are – still searching, still wondering why it's not clicking for you like it seems to for everyone else.

I get it. I have been there. It's exhausting and disheartening. You might be on the brink of throwing in the towel, thinking this online money-making thing just isn't for you. But hold up. What if I told you this book could be the game-changer? That it might just shift the way you think about making money online?

I'm not going to throw fancy words or big promises at you. But here's the deal – this guide, the one you're holding right now, it worked for me. And I've seen it work for loads of other folks too. It's not magic. It's about taking action, the right kind of action. You've got to be willing to roll up your sleeves and dive in. Think of Nike's slogan, "Just Do It." That's the mindset to have. Not just trying, but doing.

So, how about a deal? Promise me you'll give this a real shot. No half-hearted attempts. Dive into this guide, apply what you learn, and really go for it. Who knows, this might just be the book that turns it all around for you.

Here's to hoping "Make Money with Zero Cost" is the last book you'll need on your journey to making money online. Let's get started.

DISCLAIMER

This book, "Make Money with Zero Cost," is intended for informational and educational purposes only. The author and publisher have made every effort to ensure the accuracy and reliability of the information provided within these pages. However, the strategies, tips, and suggestions contained in this book are not guaranteed to produce income, as individual results may vary significantly based on a range of factors, including but not limited to personal effort, market conditions, and individual skills.

The methods and information presented in this book are the author's personal experiences and insights. Readers are advised to exercise their own judgment and conduct thorough research before engaging in any business or investment activities. The author and publisher are not responsible for any losses or damages that may result from the application of information contained in this book.

Please be aware that the digital arbitrage landscape is ever-evolving, and while the author has made every effort to keep the information current, some strategies and platforms may change over time.

By continuing to read this book, you acknowledge and agree that you are using the information provided at your own risk.

INTRODUCTION

Embarking on the Digital Arbitrage Journey

Welcome to a world where the digital marketplace is not just a platform, but a landscape of opportunities. My name is Benjamin Lang, and I'm here to guide you through the intricate yet rewarding path of making money online with no initial investment. This isn't just a guide; it's a journey we embark on together, where I share not only the steps but also the experiences and lessons that have shaped my success in digital products and services arbitrage.

Like many of you, my journey began with curiosity and a bit of skepticism. The online world is vast, and the idea of making a substantial income through digital arbitrage seemed almost too good to be true. But as I delved deeper, I discovered a realm teeming with possibilities, and I realized that the only thing standing between me and success was the willingness to take action.

I remember the early days, the initial trials and errors, and the exhilarating moment of my first successful transaction. Each step was a learning experience, teaching me not just about the tactics of digital arbitrage, but also about the mindset needed to thrive in this space.

Here's the beauty of digital arbitrage, and why we call it zero cost: the client pays us first, then we use the client's money to buy from the seller, and finally, we deliver the products to the client. This process minimizes our upfront investment, allowing us to operate with minimal financial risk. It's a strategy that has opened doors to endless opportunities without needing a hefty initial capital.

In this book, I will share everything I've learned - the strategies that worked, the pitfalls to avoid, and the insights gained from each success and setback. Whether you're a seasoned digital marketer or a newcomer eager to explore new avenues, these pages are crafted to provide you with a blueprint for success.

So, let's turn the page and start this exciting journey together.

UNDERSTANDING DIGITAL PRODUCTS ARBITRAGE

The Art of Turning Digital Opportunities into Profits

Digital products arbitrage might sound complex, but at its core, it's beautifully simple. It's about buying digital goods or services at a lower price and selling them at a higher price. The difference? That's your profit. But it's more than just buy low, sell high. It's about understanding the digital landscape, identifying opportunities, and making smart, informed decisions.

My First Encounter with Digital Arbitrage

I remember my initial foray into this world. It was a mix of excitement and nervousness. The concept was straightforward, but applying it seemed daunting. I began by exploring various online platforms, from forums to marketplaces. Each platform was a new world, with its unique rules and opportunities.

I learned quickly that success in digital arbitrage isn't just about finding the cheapest deals. It's about understanding what people want, what they value, and how to deliver it to them efficiently. It's about trust, reliability, and building relationships - not just with buyers but also with sellers.

Why Digital Products?

The beauty of digital products lies in their nature. They're scalable, easy to distribute, and often, they have a global market. Whether it's a software license key, a streaming service account, or an online course, digital products are in high demand. And the best part? There's no need for physical inventory, which cuts down on overhead costs and simplifies logistics.

The Potential of Digital Arbitrage

The potential in digital arbitrage is immense. It's not just about making a quick buck; it's about building a sustainable business. Over time, I discovered that with the right approach, digital arbitrage could be more than a side hustle. It could be a primary source of income, offering flexibility and the opportunity to scale.

PLATFORMS FOR ARBITRAGE

Navigating the Digital Marketplaces

In the world of digital arbitrage, your success hinges on knowing where to look. The internet is teeming with platforms offering a plethora of opportunities, but not all are created equal. Here, I'll share the key platforms I've used and the unique aspects of each that can help you in your arbitrage journey.

MPGH.net: A Goldmine for Bargains

My journey with MPGH.net was nothing short of eye-opening. This site, known for its incredibly low prices, was a revelation. I remember feeling like a kid in a candy store, browsing through the endless options available. But it's not just about the low prices; it's about understanding what sells and how to present it to your buyers.

eBay: The Old Reliable

eBay is a familiar name, but its potential for digital arbitrage is often underestimated. I've found eBay to be particularly useful for specific items like VPNs and software keys. The trick lies in knowing how to search effectively and understanding the pricing dynamics. Remember, eBay is more than just an auction site; it's a rich resource for arbitrage.

Nulled.to: The Untapped Resource

When I first stumbled upon Nulled.to, I knew I had found something special. This forum offers a vast range of digital products, from streaming accounts to gift cards. The key here is to navigate the 'Premium Sellers' section for reliable deals. My experience with their autobuy features has been nothing short of smooth and profitable.

Exploring Beyond the Mainstream

While MPGH.net, eBay, and Nulled.to are my go-to platforms, the digital world is vast. Sites like Bitify.Com and various other forums offer unique opportunities for those willing to explore. Each platform has its quirks and learning them can give you an edge.

EFFECTIVE STRATEGIES FOR RESELLING

Mastering the Art of the Deal

Reselling digital products is more than just a transaction; it's about understanding market dynamics, building customer trust, and creating value. Here, I'll share some of the strategies that have helped me turn reselling into a profitable venture.

Pricing: The Balancing Act

One of the first lessons I learned in reselling was the importance of pricing. It's a delicate balance between profitability and competitiveness. My approach has always been to offer a fair price that reflects the value of the product while ensuring a healthy profit margin. Remember, overpricing can drive customers away, but underpricing can undervalue your service.

Customer Relations: The Key to Repeat Business

Building a rapport with customers has been instrumental in

my success. I make it a point to communicate clearly, deliver promptly, and address any concerns swiftly. A happy customer is not just a repeat customer but also a source of referrals. I've found that treating each customer interaction with care and professionalism goes a long way.

Product Selection: Finding Your Niche

While it's tempting to jump on every product that seems profitable, I've learned that specialization can be more effective. By focusing on a niche, you can build expertise and a loyal customer base. For me, identifying a few key products that I was passionate about and that had a steady demand was a game-changer.

Managing Risks and Disputes

In digital reselling, disputes are inevitable. How you handle them can make all the difference. I always advocate for resolving issues amicably, offering refunds when necessary, and learning from each incident to improve the process. Keeping a clean record, especially with payment processors like PayPal, is crucial.

KICKSTARTING YOUR DIGITAL ARBITRAGE JOURNEY

Taking the First Steps

Embarking on your journey in digital arbitrage can feel overwhelming, but it doesn't have to be. Here's a straightforward path to get you started, beginning with the resources closest to you and gradually expanding your reach.

1. Start with Friends and Family

Your personal network is a great starting point. They're people who trust you, and you understand their needs and interests. Begin by offering them products and services that are part of everyday life, but at a better price. It's a win-win situation where they get something with a better price and you earn some money from that.

- Premium Netflix Account: Ask if they're interested in a premium Netflix account at a discounted rate. It's something many people use and can be an easy sell.
- Antivirus Licenses: Offer legitimate antivirus licenses at

a lower price. It's a practical item that most people need for their digital security.
- Discounted Products: Know someone who loves Nike? See if they're interested in getting their next pair of shoes with a discount code.

2. Engage in Online Communities

Once you're comfortable, take it to the next level by sharing posts in online forums and Facebook groups. Here, targeting is key. Make sure your offers align with the interests of the group members.

- Tech and Business Forums: Offer VPN services, web hosting, or SEO tools on 'make money online' forums or groups.
- Special Interest Groups: Join groups with specific interests, like wine lovers, and offer relevant deals like wine vouchers.
- Travel Enthusiasts: Share offers for discounted flight tickets, travel coupons, or mileage deals in travel and leisure groups.

3. Develop Your Own Website

With some experience under your belt, create a website to showcase and sell a variety of products. This gives you a professional platform and makes it easier for customers to browse and buy.

- Diversify Your Offerings: Include different types of products that appeal to a broader audience.

- Promote Your Website: Use your personal network and the online communities you're a part of to drive traffic to your site.

4. Invest in Online Advertising

Ready to reach a wider audience? Online advertising can be a powerful tool. Start with a modest budget and focus on platforms where your target audience is most active.

- Facebook Ads: Great for reaching a diverse audience with specific interests.
- Google Ads: Use this to capture people who are actively searching for the products you offer.
- Twitter and Bing Ads: Don't overlook these platforms, as they can also drive significant traffic depending on your target market.

SPECIFIC PRODUCTS
AND SERVICES
FOR ARBITRAGE

Identifying Lucrative Opportunities

The digital marketplace is vast, but not all products are created equal when it comes to arbitrage opportunities. Over the years, I've honed in on specific products and services that offer the best potential for profit. Here, I'll share insights into these categories and why they stand out.

Streaming Accounts and Software Keys

One of the first niches I explored was streaming accounts and software keys. The demand for these products is consistently high, and the profit margins can be substantial. Streaming services like Netflix and software like Microsoft Office are always in demand. The key is sourcing these products at a significantly lower cost, which I found feasible through platforms like MPGH.net and eBay.

Educational and Entertainment Accounts

Another area ripe for arbitrage is educational and entertainment accounts. Services like Lynda.com or premium sports streaming passes have a dedicated audience. I learned early on that these accounts could be sourced inexpensively and sold at a markup without pricing them out of reach for the average consumer.

VPN and Internet Security Services

VPNs and internet security services are not only popular but also offer the benefit of recurring sales. Customers often need these services for extended periods, opening the door for repeat business. My strategy has been to focus on reliability and trust, ensuring that customers feel secure in their purchases.

Gaming Accounts and Digital Currencies

The gaming industry is a goldmine for arbitrage. From gaming accounts for popular games like Fortnite to digital currencies used in these games, the opportunities are vast. My approach has been to understand the gaming community's needs and cater to them, often leading to quick and profitable sales.

ADVANCED TECHNIQUES AND TIPS

Refining Your Strategy for Maximum Gain

Digital arbitrage, while accessible, can be elevated to new heights with advanced techniques. These strategies, which I've refined over time, can help you maximize profits, expand your reach, and operate more efficiently.

Leveraging Regional Differences

One of the most powerful techniques I've discovered is exploiting regional differences in product availability and pricing. For instance, a product unavailable or priced higher on eBay.com might be found for less on a regional eBay site, like eBay.es. This approach requires a bit of extra research but can open up a wealth of opportunities that others might overlook.

Utilizing Group Buys for High-Value Products

Group Buys (GBs) are a fantastic way to access high-value products like expensive courses or software tools at a fraction of their cost. The key here is to organize or participate in GBs judiciously. It's about balancing the desire for profit with the need to offer genuine value to participants. Remember, transparency and fairness in GBs can build your reputation and trust, which are invaluable in the long run.

Exploring Internet Marketing Tools

The world of Internet Marketing (IM) tools offers vast opportunities for arbitrage. Websites like seotoolsagency.com and seogb.org provide access to premium tools at affordable rates. Reselling access or reports generated from these tools can be highly profitable. I've found that offering tailored services based on these tools, such as detailed SEO reports, adds value to clients while generating significant returns.

Maximizing Profit with Affiliate Programs

Don't overlook the potential of affiliate programs. Platforms that offer these programs can be a steady source of passive income. By promoting products or services related to your arbitrage business, you can earn commissions on top of your direct sales profits. This approach requires some marketing savvy but can significantly boost your overall earnings.

RISK MANAGEMENT AND SAFETY

Safeguarding Your Business in the Digital Marketplace

In the realm of digital arbitrage, managing risks and ensuring the safety of your transactions are paramount. My experiences have taught me the importance of being vigilant, especially when dealing with payment processors like PayPal.

Keeping Your PayPal Account Safe

PayPal is a popular choice for digital transactions, but it comes with its own set of challenges. To keep your account in good standing, it's vital to understand and adhere to their Terms of Service. Here are some tips I've learned along the way:

- Manual Transactions Over Automation: While automated stores like Selly.gg or Shoppy.gg are convenient, they often display item names in transactions, which can be a red flag. I recommend handling transactions manually to keep the details discreet.

- Clear Communication with Buyers: Ask your buyers not to mention the item name in the PayPal note. This small step can go a long way in keeping your transactions under the radar.

- Handling Disputes Proactively: Avoiding disputes on PayPal is crucial. Encourage your buyers to contact you directly for any issues. If a dispute does arise, it's often better to offer a refund than to engage in a prolonged conflict.

- Using Alternative Payment Methods: To further reduce risk, consider accepting payments in cryptocurrencies like Bitcoin or Ethereum. This not only diversifies your payment options but also adds a layer of security and anonymity.

Navigating Disputes and Refunds

Disputes and refunds are inevitable in any business. The key is to handle them gracefully. Here's how:

- Immediate Response: Address any issues or complaints as soon as they arise. This proactive approach often diffuses potential disputes.

- Fair Refund Policy: Be clear about your refund policy. Sometimes, issuing a refund is a better option than risking a tarnished reputation or a banned account.

- Building Trust: Consistent, fair handling of disputes builds trust with your customer base, leading to more business and fewer issues in the long run.

SETTING UP YOUR BUSINESS

Laying the Groundwork for Your Digital Arbitrage Venture

Starting an online business in digital arbitrage requires more than just understanding the market and products; it involves setting a solid foundation. Here, I'll walk you through the essential steps to establish your business effectively.

1. Establishing an Online Presence

The first step is to create your online storefront. This could be on established marketplaces, your website, or even on social media platforms. The key is to choose a medium that aligns with your target market. For example, if you're selling gaming accounts, platforms like gaming forums or social media groups can be ideal.

2. Legal Considerations and Compliance

Understanding and adhering to legal requirements is crucial. This includes complying with the terms of service of the platforms you use, as well as any local business regulations. While arbitrage is a legitimate business model, ensuring that you operate within legal boundaries is essential to maintain credibility and avoid potential issues.

3. Payment Processing and Security

Setting up secure and reliable payment processing is critical. Explore options beyond PayPal, like Stripe or cryptocurrency payments, to diversify and secure your transactions. Ensuring payment security not only protects you but also builds trust with your customers.

4. Developing a Customer Service Strategy

Excellent customer service can set you apart in the digital marketplace. Develop a strategy that includes prompt responses, clear communication, and a fair approach to disputes and refunds. Remember, a satisfied customer is more likely to return and recommend your service.

SCALING YOUR BUSINESS

Expanding Beyond the Initial Success

Once you've established your digital arbitrage business and started to see some success, the next step is scaling up. Scaling is about growing your business in a sustainable way, increasing your profits while maintaining quality and customer satisfaction.

1. Diversifying Your Product Range

One effective way to scale is by diversifying the products you offer. While it's important to start with a niche, as your business grows, so should your product range. This doesn't mean losing focus but rather understanding related markets and customer needs. For example, if you started with streaming accounts, consider expanding into related digital products like e-books or software.

2. Exploring New Markets

Expanding into new markets is another key strategy for scaling. This could mean targeting customers in different geographical regions or exploring new online platforms. Each market has its unique characteristics and demands, so research and understanding these nuances are crucial.

3. Building a Strong Brand and Online Presence

As your business grows, so should your brand. A strong brand helps in attracting new customers and retaining existing ones. Invest in developing a professional online presence, whether it's through a well-designed website, active social media engagement, or online marketing.

4. Automating and Streamlining Operations

Efficiency is key when scaling your business. Look into automating certain aspects of your operations, like customer communications or order processing. This frees up your time to focus on growth strategies and new opportunities.

5. Collaborating and Networking

Never underestimate the power of networking and collaboration. Building relationships with other sellers, participating in online communities, and collaborating on joint ventures can open up new avenues for growth and expansion.

CONCLUSION

As we reach the end of this guide, I hope you feel equipped with the knowledge and strategies to start your journey in digital products and services arbitrage. The path to success in this field is as exciting as it is challenging, but the rewards are well worth the effort.

Key Takeaways

- Start with Action: The most important step is to start. Take action, learn from your experiences, and don't be afraid to experiment.
- Understand Your Products and Market: Success comes from knowing your products and understanding your market. Always stay informed and adaptable.
- Build Relationships: Whether it's with your customers or other sellers, building strong, trustworthy relationships is key.
- Stay Compliant and Ethical: Always operate within the bounds of legality and ethics. This not only protects your business but also builds your reputation.
- Scale Smartly: When scaling your business, do so thoughtfully and sustainably. Diversify your offerings and explore new markets, but maintain the quality and customer service that got you started.

Final Words of Encouragement

Your journey in digital arbitrage will be unique, filled with its own set of challenges and triumphs. Remember, every successful entrepreneur started somewhere, and with persistence, adaptability, and a willingness to learn, you too can achieve remarkable success.

I wish you the best of luck as you embark on this exciting path. Remember, the digital marketplace is vast and ever-evolving, and it's filled with opportunities for those willing to seek them out. Go forth with confidence, creativity, and a commitment to excellence, and the world of digital arbitrage will open its doors to you.